For Guinness, the best of cats
FMW
For Barbara and Derek
VJ-O

For permission to reproduce copyright material, acknowledgement and thanks are due to the following:
Daniel Payne for 'I Met a Cat'; Monica Shannon and Doubleday & Co. Inc. for 'Only My Opinion'
from *Goose Grass Rhymes;* Clare Rhodes for 'You can't catch me!';
Thirza Wakley and Unwin Hyman for 'The Mouse' from
The Book of a Thousand Poems; Mary Ann Hobermann and Russell and Volkening Inc. for 'Tiger'
from *Hello and Goodbye* published by Little Brown Inc.
Every effort has been made to trace copyright but if any omissions have been made please
let us know in order that we may put them right in the next edition.

 **Children's Publishing**

This compilation copyright © Fiona Waters 1990, 2003
Illustrations copyright © Vanessa Julian-Ottie 1990, 2003
First published in 1990 by Hodder and Stoughton Children's Books

This edition published in the United States of America in 2003 by
Gingham Dog Press
an imprint of McGraw-Hill Children's Publishing,
a Division of The McGraw-Hill Companies
8787 Orion Place
Columbus, Ohio 43240-4027

www.MHkids.com

Printed in China.

0-7696-3188-6

1 2 3 4 5 6 7 8 9 10 MP 09 08 07 06 05 04 03

The **McGraw·Hill** Companies

Whiskers and Paws

Poems chosen by Fiona Waters

Illustrated by Vanessa Julian-Ottie

GINGHAM DOG
PRESS

Columbus, Ohio

I Met a Cat

I met a cat and he was magic
So he played a fiddle for me
And I danced with him to the music
Until it was half past three.

Daniel Payne

Only My Opinion

Is a caterpillar ticklish?
Well, it's always my belief
That he giggles as he wiggles
Across a hairy leaf.

Monica Shannon

Polar Bear

The secret of the polar bear
Is that he wears long underwear.

Gail Kredenser

Higglety, Pigglety, Pop!

Higglety, pigglety, pop!
The dog has eaten the mop;
The pig's in a hurry,
The cat's in a flurry,
Higglety, pigglety, pop!

Anonymous

You Can't Catch Me!

I'm a velvety mole
My home is a hole
I'm not very big
But I do like to dig
I'll spoil your lawn
But I'm gone by dawn
I chuckle with glee
For you can't catch me!

Clare Rhodes

The Mouse

There's such a tiny little mouse
Living safely in my house.
Out at night he'll softly creep,
When everyone is fast asleep.
But always in the light of day
He softly, sofly creeps away.

Thirza Wakley

Rat a Tat Tat

Rat a tat tat, who is that?
Only Grandma's pussy cat.
What do you want?
A pint of milk.
Where's your money?
In my pocket.
Where's your pocket?
I forgot it.
Oh, you silly pussy cat!

Anonymous

Hickety Pickety

Hickety Pickety
My black hen.
She lays eggs
For gentlemen.
Sometimes nine
And sometimes ten.
Hickety Pickety
My black hen.

Anonymous

Tiger

I'm a tiger
Striped with fur
   Don't come near
     Or I might Grrr
      Don't come near
       Or I might growl
        Don't come near
         Or I might BITE!

Mary Ann Hobermann

He and She

He was a rat, and she was a rat,
And down in one hole they did dwell,
And both were as black as a witch's cat,
And they loved one another well.

Anonymous

White Sheep

White sheep, white sheep
On a blue hill,
When the wind stops
You all stand still.
You all run away
When the winds blow;
White sheep, white sheep,
Where do you go?

Anonymous